W9-CHQ-789

SEEDS
FROM A SECRET GARDEN

By Gertrude Hyde
Illustrated by Katharine Barnwell
Designed by Gina Federico

PETER PAUPER PRESS, INC.
WHITE PLAINS • NEW YORK

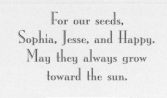

For our seeds,
Sophia, Jesse, and Happy.
May they always grow
toward the sun.

Cover and seed packet illustration
by Katharine Barnwell

Copyright © 1997
Peter Pauper Press, Inc.
202 Mamaroneck Avenue
White Plains, NY 10601
All rights reserved
ISBN 0-88088-890-3
Printed in Singapore
7 6 5 4 3 2

Seeds From A Secret Garden

To everything there is a
Season. May these
seeds bloom beautiful

for you,

Great Love

Maryleue

12/98

Introduction

*Your secret garden is next
to your heart.
It shelters your innermost thoughts.
Recognize the key, unlock the door.*

Any garden can be a secret
garden. A place to watch the
miracle of a seed breaking through
the soil, unfurling its foliage, tum-
bling its petals in hues and colors

that are the envy of any artist. A garden of safety and familiarity closing off what you wish to keep at a distance and letting in that which gives you comfort and sustenance. A place to think or perhaps not to think at all but to feel nature's hum. A place to dig, to pinch back or prune, and to await renewed growth within.

Follow the paths through your secret garden. As the seasons turn, watch spring's carpet of daffodils give way to curtains of lilac blossoms, and ruffled peonies move into summer's breathless rose, delicate irises, and big-faced sunflower babies in bonnets.

Sit on the stone bench as the late summer asters fade a little each day, signaling the turning of the leaves, as the secret garden moves toward putting on its winter veil. Unheard and unseen below the hush of the snow, next spring's plants are already preparing beneath the surface for another cycle of emergence.

— G. H.

A secret garden is within you and within your mind's sight.
Plant the garden so that you may grow.

Planting is the act of an optimist.

The garden renews itself through change.

The garden reflects your
accord with nature,
and your disagreements.

You will often fall in love
in your secret garden,
and no love formed there
goes unrequited.

Any garden can grow
to be a secret garden;
the stuff of dreams lies
within the seeds.

Any garden can be
a secret garden,
as whispers pass
between you and the
natural world.

In the garden some forms of life
hug the ground.

Others hold fast to the underside of
the leaves or wriggle with
determination through the soil.

All return something in kind
to replenish what they
have taken.

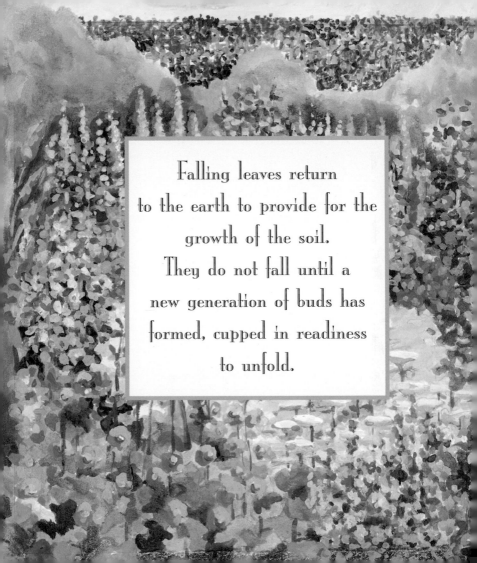

Falling leaves return
to the earth to provide for the
growth of the soil.
They do not fall until a
new generation of buds has
formed, cupped in readiness
to unfold.

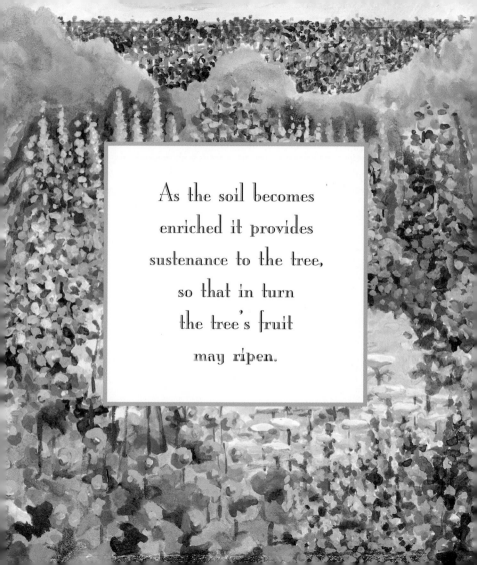

As the soil becomes
enriched it provides
sustenance to the tree,
so that in turn
the tree's fruit
may ripen.

If your purpose is to dig a hole
in the ground, do so.
If you intend to place a plant
in that hole,
you must first feed the soil.

———————

Cup the soil in your hands
and bring it to your face.
Receive the scent of life
that has preceded you.

Nature's colors are the
gardener's palette,
and her soil the
gardener's canvas
backlit by the moods
of the sky.

Renewal is the measure of new growth.

Observe your garden and you touch upon life's primal force.

Within your mind
are the seeds of infinite
possibilities;
when the seed breaks
the surface the possibilities
become unlimited.

Long journeys
require very few steps
in the secret garden.

Each seed is a
journey to discovery.

Each plant is a measure of
that journey's progress.

E*ach fruit is sustenance*
for the body.

E*ach flower*
is a face of discovery
turning toward
the full light
of the sun.

Everything
that happens in this garden
has meaning;
Carry its essence with you
everywhere.

To everything
there is a season,
and within each season
are the seasons of bloom.
Embrace each
plant within its season
and cherish each
season for its part in the
fullness of the cycle.

Fog,
rain, storms,
snow, frost, ice, water—
time moves them all
through the
garden.

A
garden
that is declared
"finished"
is on the edge
of extinction.

A gardener
can provide a path
that will take you from one point
to another.
What you choose to see
while on that path
is in your hands.

The vines move
with apparent
weightlessness
in the breeze,
yet are securely
rooted in the
earth.

N_o branch
ever broke from
bending
with the
wind.

The quality of light,
the perceived color of a flower,
the shadows on the ground,
change with the attitude
of the sun.
Is it any wonder
that our moods shift with the
play of the changing light?

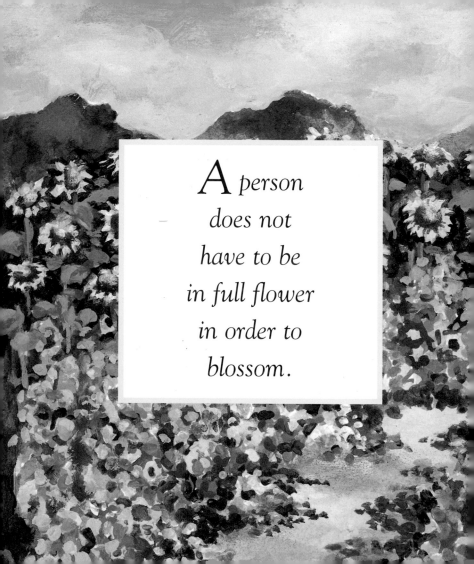

A person
does not
have to be
in full flower
in order to
blossom.

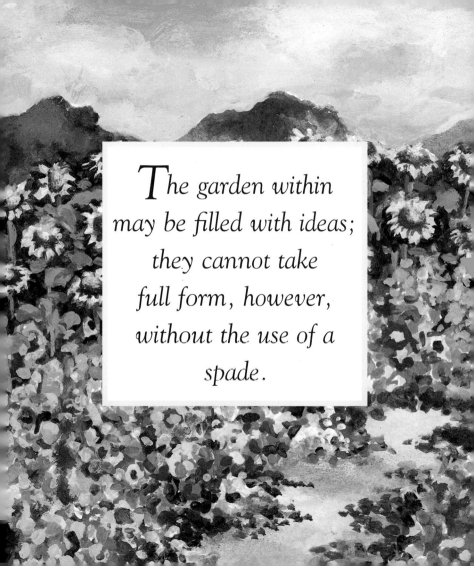

The garden within may be filled with ideas; they cannot take full form, however, without the use of a spade.

Even
a master gardener
is humbled
by the emergence
of a blade of
grass.

A tree
marks the center
of paradise;
stand
beneath its
outstretched
arms.

The tree
where mankind
was born
still stands.

Pilgrims of all sorts
come to the
secret garden —
to pollinate, to drop seeds,
to drink, and to
find shade.

To find the source
you must work your way
back down below
the surface.
Tend to the roots.

If you
are seeing clearly
there are no forests,
only trees.

The tree's rings
tell a tale of time.

Knowledge
of what has come before
is served by reading the rings
even before counting them.

The longer that you sit
in the garden
the better you will see.
The more clearly you see
the more you will
understand.

Water
is at the source
of everything;
the plants
embrace it and
guard it.

The contemplation of a
single droplet of water on
a flower's petal is an entryway
to the sublime.

The lotus unfolds above the water;
its strength, however, is anchored below.

A secret garden
is not a microcosm of
the world.
It is the world.

Secret Gardens
are cradles of memories
of ancestors
and childhood.

There are memories here
of ancestors who sat
on this bench
and watched this rose
climb, and flower,
and decline, and weather
the winters and return

to climb and flower
season upon season ago
and to remember
their childhood memories,
and their ancestors
who sat on this bench
season upon season ago.
Secret gardens are cradles of
memories and nurseries of
dreams.